God, Can You Hear Me?

JUSTINE SIMMONS

Paintings by Robert Papp

HarperCollins*Publishers*
Amistad

To God, the head of my life—
and to my wonderful husband, children, and
parents, who are my inspiration in all things,
including this book.

Amistad is an imprint of HarperCollins Publishers.

God, Can You Hear Me?
Text copyright © 2007 by Justine Simmons
Illustrations copyright © 2007 by Robert Papp

Manufactured in China.

Library of Congress Cataloging-in-Publication Data is available.
ISBN-10: 0-06-115397-4 (trade bdg.) — ISBN-13: 978-0-06-115397-6 (trade bdg.)

Designed by Stephanie Bart-Horvath
1 2 3 4 5 6 7 8 9 10

First Edition

Dear Reader,

One day my son Daniel, who is normally cheerful and outgoing, seemed burdened and sad. Clearly something was weighing heavily on his heart, but when his father Joey and I went to talk to him, he didn't want to discuss his problem with us. His father and I have always taught our children to turn to God for help when they have a problem that they can't solve on their own.

That night, without telling us, Daniel wrote a letter to God. The following morning we greeted Daniel as usual. What was ailing him came up in our conversation, and we were able to help him feel much better. In Daniel's mind, the letter to God worked! From that point forward, Daniel knew that God could hear and would answer his prayers. This was when I realized how truly important the connection to God is, not only for adults, but also for young souls.

We would like to believe that as parents and grandparents, teachers and spiritual counselors, and extended family, we can provide our children with answers to everything. But we sometimes forget how challenging our children's lives have become. Though we do the best we can, sometimes our answers aren't good enough to calm our children's fears or to steer them in the right direction.

This realization prompted me to write *God, Can You Hear Me?* I want all children to know that there exists another powerful source of inspiration and guidance that they can depend on when they need help. This sense of strength begins in their hearts and reassures them that God will always watch out for them.

Enjoy,

Justine

*You can ask God anything. It can be about your family,
your friends, or whatever is on your mind. These are some of
the questions I've heard kids share with God.*

I wish I had a baby sister or brother because I have no one to play with.

God, can you hear me?

Everyone gets lonely sometimes. As an only child, you are just as special as children with brothers and sisters. You can still have fun with your friends and family, reading books, and playing with your toys.

My friend is in a wheelchair. Did she do something wrong?

God, can you hear me?

Some people have physical disabilities.
But that doesn't mean they did something
wrong or bad. Treat your friend as you
would treat anyone else—with kindness.

My friend lives with her mom and dad, but I live with just one parent.

Why can't I be like everyone else?

God, can you hear me?

All families are different. You don't need
to be like anyone else. Instead, enjoy all
the love in your family and in your life.

Sometimes kids make fun of the color of my skin. It makes me feel bad.
God, can you hear me?

God loves us all, no matter what color
we are. He chose beautiful colors for
each of us. Be thankful and proud of the
color he made you.

Grandma died. Is she really gone forever?

God, can you hear me?

Grandma is no longer with us, but if you cherish the memories of the time you spent together, you will always keep her alive in your heart.

Mommy and Daddy argue all the time. Do they still love each other?

God, can you hear me?

Mommy and Daddy may argue, but they still love each other. And they love you, too.

I wish I were thinner so I'd look more like my friends.

God, can you hear me?

God loves you just the way you are, no matter what your body shape or size is. Love yourself, and then others will see what is special about you.

When Mommy raises her voice at me, does she still love me?

God, can you hear me?

Just because Mommy raises her voice
doesn't mean she doesn't love you. She
just wants the best for you.

My dog Sparky ran away. Will he be okay?

God, can you hear me?

Sparky is so adorable and clever. I'm sure whoever finds him will love him and take good care of him.

Mommy and Daddy are not the same color.
Does that make me different from my friends?
God, can you hear me?

What's important is that your parents
love you, and that you love yourself.

My parents can't afford to buy me designer clothing. Am I still cool?

God, can you hear me?

What makes you cool is who you are
on the inside, not what you wear on
the outside.

I have a new stepfamily. Will I fit in?

God, can you hear me?

A stepfamily can be cool because now
you have two families to share things
with, two families to love. Don't forget,
no matter what kind of family you have,
there is always God's love.

❧❧

Maybe you have also wondered about some of the questions in this book.
Remember, you can share everything with God.

❧❧

*I*n the pages you've just read, children go to God when they are missing some-one special in their life, such as their grandmother or even their dog, or when they are concerned with their body image and fitting in. Perhaps you are experiencing the same things as the kids in this book. Or maybe you have different questions for God.

Whether you feel similar to the kids in this book or want to talk to God about what's happening in your school, on your block, or in your home, you should know that he cares and wants to hear from you. Make your questions specific. The more you call upon God for guidance, the more help you will get.

As a child you are blessed to have the opportunity to create a wonderful friend-ship with God for the rest of your life. Take advantage of it.

Justine